The BOY WHO NEVER GAVE UP

STEPHEN CURRY

The Children's Book

By Anthony Curcio

www.sportivabooks.com

After dinner one night, a boy sat down to do his homework.
He just sat there, staring at the table, daydreaming...

"Mom, do you think I could play in the NBA like dad?"

The boy's mother looked at him with a smile and said,
"If you practice enough I think anything is possible, but
for now you need to finish your homework."

When the boy finished his homework he went outside
and did what he always did. He played basketball.

The boy played other sports too,
but he *loved* basketball.

Basketball was the only sport that really made him dream.

The small boy dreamed of one day playing in the NBA.

"Starting at guard, number thirty... Stephen Currrrrrrrrrrrry!"

"Yaaaaa! Ohhhhhh! Awwwwww!" Stephen yelled in his best crowd-screaming voice.

That's me!

"I look forward to going to the NBA when I get older and I would like to get my college education."

Stephen Curry (age 13)

2002 Queensway Christian yearbook

Stephen in 2002 (8ᵗʰ Grade)

The problem was, Stephen was too small and too short. All the kids at school *just knew* that he was too little for the NBA... except for Stephen of course.

"One day, I'm going to play in the NBA just like my dad."

"Hahahahahahaha!" the other kids at school laughed.

"There is *no way* that you'll play in the NBA like your dad."

"He is big and strong and you are small and weak!"

Despite his size, little Stephen kept playing. He became very skilled at dribbling and passing, but because the hoop was so high and he was so short, it was difficult for Stephen to shoot the ball when he was guarded closely.

He was only 5'6" tall and 125lbs as a sophomore in high school. Because he was smaller, Stephen had to work harder and practice more.

One day, Stephen's dad was watching him shoot baskets outside. He noticed how hard Stephen tried to always get better.

"Son, you have more heart and determination than any other player I have seen. I know you are smaller than other players so I want to teach you something that will help."

"The other kids may be taller but if you bring up your shot and learn to shoot faster, they won't be able to stop you."

Stephen did what he always did - he practiced.
It wasn't easy changing the way he shot, but he kept
working every day on what his dad had taught him.
Although, it wasn't work to Stephen because he loved
basketball. When he practiced he still dreamed of
playing in the NBA.

"Starting at guard, number thirty...Stephen Currrrry!"

The following year, all of his hard work showed on the court. His dad was right, the other players *weren't* able to stop him.

Stephen led his high school team to three conference titles, earning himself several honors, including being voted one of the best players in the state!

Stephen graduated from high school and was thinking about where he wanted to go to college.

He only wanted to go to one school, Virginia Tech, where his dad had played.

Stephen *knew* he could play there too. All he needed was for them to give him a chance.

Dear Stephen,

Thank you so much for your interest in our school and basketball program. Unfortunately we are unable to offer you a scholarship.

Best of luck to you,

Dear Stephen,

I have watched you play on several occasions and I am impressed. You are a great player but just as important, you never seem to give up fighting, regardless of the challenges you are up against. I would be honored if you would play for me at Davidson College and have a scholarship for you.

Sincerely,

Coach McKillop

This is Coach Bob

But they didn't. Virginia Tech and many other schools didn't think Stephen could play on their teams. They thought he was just too small and not strong enough. Except for one coach at one very small college.

His name was Bob and he was the coach at Davidson College. Coach Bob saw what no one else could see. "Wait until you see Stephen Curry," he told everyone.

Stephen Curry could not be stopped. He led his team to victory over schools that were *ten times* the size of Davidson College, all the way to the Elite Eight.

Coach Bob was right - wait until you see Stephen play!

Stephen broke many records and won several awards. He even led the *entire* country in points scored per game!

College Statistics	Averages				Season Awards
Year in College	Points Per Game	Rebounds Per Game	Assists Per Game	Steals Per Game	Major Awards For Season
Freshman	21.5	4.6	2.8	1.8	Conference Freshman of the Year
Sophomore	25.9	4.6	2.9	2.1	Second-Team All-American
Senior	28.6	4.4	5.6	2.5	First-Team All-American

People who watched Stephen play in college started to see what Coach Bob had seen all along. Many were beginning to believe what Stephen had always believed about himself.

But there were still many people that said Stephen was just too small to play in the NBA. They said he got lucky, that he wasn't strong enough, that he wasn't good enough. They just kept talking and talking.

But Stephen didn't listen.

He was too busy winning the NBA's Most Valuable Player Award *twice*, leading the league in scoring and steals, taking his team to NBA Championships and pretty much breaking every 3-point record that has ever existed.

Stephen was told he was too short in high school, too weak in college, and not good enough to play in the NBA.

He has proven that never giving up is *more* important than being the biggest, the tallest or even the strongest. But most importantly, Stephen Curry has proven that...

Dreams come true!

NEVER GIVE UP

The Boy Who Never Gave Up

www.sportivabooks.com

Printed in Great Britain
by Amazon